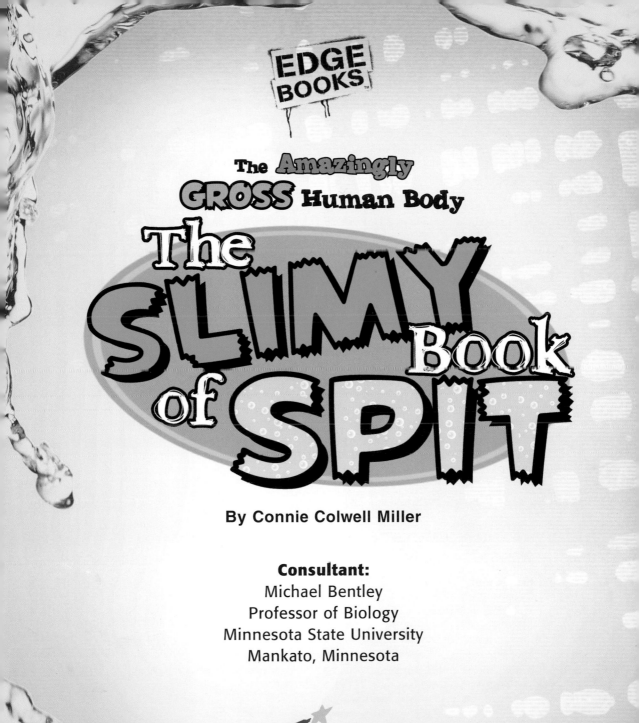

EDGE BOOKS™

The Amazingly GROSS Human Body

The SLIMY Book of SPIT

By Connie Colwell Miller

Consultant:
Michael Bentley
Professor of Biology
Minnesota State University
Mankato, Minnesota

Capstone press®

Mankato, Minnesota

Edge Books are published by Capstone Press,
151 Good Counsel Drive, P.O. Box 669, Mankato, Minnesota 56002.
www.capstonepress.com

Books published by Capstone Press are manufactured with paper
containing at least 10 percent post-consumer waste.

Library of Congress Cataloging-in-Publication Data
Miller, Connie Colwell, 1976–
 The slimy book of spit / by Connie Colwell Miller.
 p. cm. — (Edge. The amazingly gross human body)
 Summary: "Describes what spit consists of, how the human body
manufactures spit, and why spit is gross" — Provided by publisher.
 Includes bibliographical references and index.
 ISBN 978-1-4296-3355-0 (library binding)
 1. Saliva — Juvenile literature. 2. Drooling — Juvenile literature. 3. Saliva
glands — Juvenile literature. I. Title. II. Series.
QP191.M55 2010
612.3'13 — dc22   2009002165

Editorial Credits
Mandy Robbins, editor; Kyle Grenz, designer; Jo Miller, media researcher

Photo Credits
Capstone Press/Karon Dubke, cover, 4, 8, 10, 11, 13 (both), 17 (both),
    18 (main image), 19, 21 (main image), 22, 24, 25, 27, 28–29 (both)
CDC/Bette Jensen, 18 (inset); Segrid McAllister, 26
Newscom/AFP Photo/Teh Eng Koon, 7
Photo Researchers, Inc/Anatomical Travelogue, 14
Shutterstock/Filipe B. Varela (pouring water design element), used throughout;
    Morgan Lane Photography, 21 (banana)

TABLE of CONTENTS

NOTHING to SPIT AT

Sleeping in class is embarrassing.
Drooling on your desk is even worse!

Launch a loogie. Drool on your pillow. Wipe slobber on your sleeve. It seems like you can do a million gross things with your spit. But did you know that spit also helps your body do some pretty important stuff?

Spit, or saliva, is a clear fluid that squirts into your mouth. Spit is mostly made of water. But it also has chemicals and **enzymes** in it that help break down food.

You may not think much about your spit. But spit helps your body in some amazing ways. Without spit, you would not be able to speak, and eating would be very difficult. In fact, you wouldn't even be able to taste your food.

enzyme a substance that helps break down food

HISTORY OF SPIT

Hundreds of years ago, spitting was common all over the world. In fact, it was considered bad manners to swallow your spit.

Over time, certain rules developed about how to spit politely. In some places, people were encouraged to spit into a cloth. In other places, covering the spit with your shoe was polite enough.

Spitting is still common in some places. The Masai people of Africa spit to show respect and goodwill. They even spit on newborn babies to wish them good luck.

The Chinese government tried to crack down on spitting before hosting the 2008 Olympics in Beijing. The government didn't want to gross out people from other countries with the common Chinese habit of spitting.

During the 2008 Olympics, signs were posted all over Beijing that read, "Please do not spit."

The SCOOP on SPIT

Your body starts producing spit
before you even put food in your mouth.

Let's say you want to eat some candy. You pop a piece into your mouth. Before you even taste it, spit goes to work.

Your tongue uses spit to taste the candy. Chemicals in the candy dissolve into your spit. Only then can your taste buds sense the sweetness. Without saliva, your tongue couldn't tell if you were chewing taffy or toenails.

Once you start to chew the candy, spit moistens it. The chemicals in your spit break down the candy into small parts. Your spit teams up with your teeth and your tongue. Together they work to mold the candy into a big lump of food and saliva called a bolus.

Finally, spit coats your throat to help the bolus slide into your esophagus. Spit also keeps your esophagus moist as the bolus moves to your stomach. There, the bolus is broken down and turned into energy for your body to use.

SAY IT, DON'T SPRAY IT!

Spit keeps your lips and tongue wet so they can move easily. Without spit, your mouth would be too dry to form the shapes it makes when you speak. You'd be like the Tin Man in *The Wizard of Oz* before Dorothy used his oil can.

Talking too much also dries out your mouth. That's why preachers and politicians keep water nearby. Once their mouths are moist, they can keep yakking!

Without spit, you would be speechless.

SPIT INSPECTION

Feeling sick? Let's inspect your spit. Spit tests are easier and less expensive to run than blood tests. Doctors use spit samples to test for certain illnesses. A person's spit can show signs of diabetes, cancer, and even AIDS.

Scientists are still working on developing more spit tests. In the future, this might mean fewer needles being jabbed into your skin and more spitting.

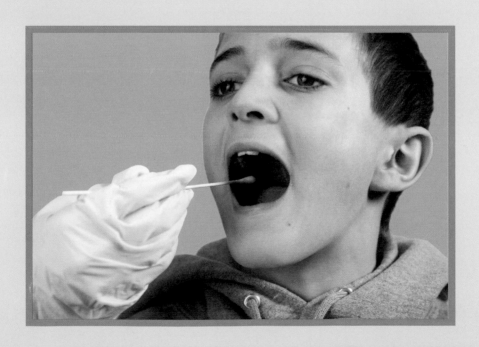

SPIT SHIELD

Spit is also a defender of your pearly whites. A good coating of spit covers your teeth at all times. This coating stands between your teeth and harmful **bacteria** that can cause cavities. Spit also washes away extra bits of food that get caught in your mouth.

Saliva can even help repair early tooth decay. To do this, chemicals in saliva calcify, or harden, a decayed spot on a tooth. When it hardens, the decayed spot can't break down any further. But don't get too excited. This doesn't mean you can skip brushing your teeth.

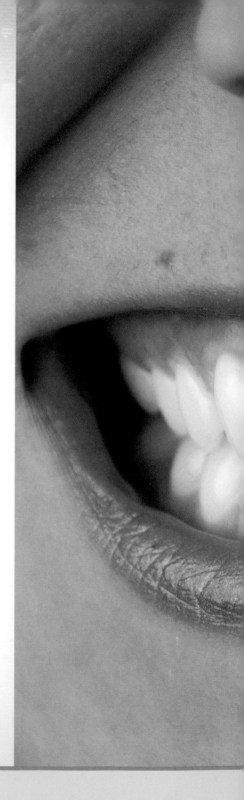

bacteria   microscopic living things; some bacteria cause tooth decay.

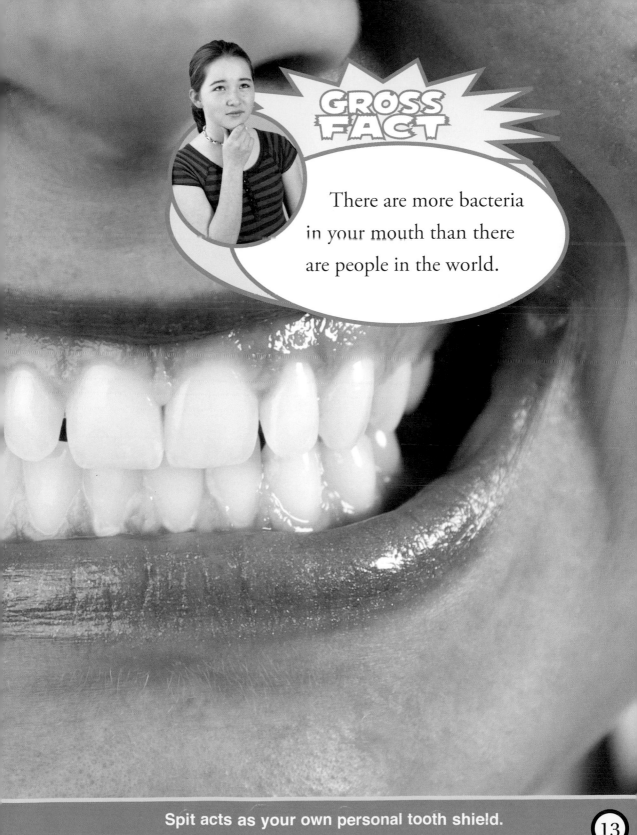

There are more bacteria in your mouth than there are people in the world.

Spit acts as your own personal tooth shield.

How SPIT HAPPENS

The gland under your tongue produces about 60 percent of your saliva.

Your body produces spit morning, noon, and night. We've already covered what this slobber does. Now let's find out how it's made.

SPIT-SHOOTERS

Your salivary glands make spit. These glands are your spit-shooters. They send spit shooting out tiny tubes into your mouth.

You have three pairs of salivary glands. The first pair shoots spit out of your cheeks. Another pair shoots spit from under your tongue. The last pair of glands shoots spit from the back of your mouth.

Most of the time, your salivary glands make the perfect amount of spit. You need just enough spit to keep your mouth moist. But too much spit will have you drooling all over your chin!

SUDDEN SPIT

Every once in a while, your salivary glands kick into overdrive. A good example is just before you vomit. Vomit is made up of disgusting chunks of chewed-up food and a great deal of **acid**. Acid can do serious damage to your teeth. When you are about to throw up, your spit-shooters ooze out extra spit to cover your teeth. The extra spit protects your teeth from all that acid.

So take that as a warning: if you ever feel a sudden flood of spit, head for the nearest toilet. You may be about to barf!

acid a strong liquid that helps break down food

GROSS FACT

Your throat doesn't have saliva to protect it from the acid in your vomit. That's why your throat burns after you puke.

Acid is also what gives vomit that sour taste.

Brushing your teeth gets rid of food particles that can attract bacteria.

NOT ENOUGH SPIT

Sometimes your body doesn't make as much spit as it needs. When you sleep, your salivary glands take a bit of a snooze too. You're still making spit, but not as much. This is why your mouth feels dry when you wake up.

Your mouth also stinks in the morning because it hasn't had enough spit to keep it clean. In the daytime, spit washes away bacteria in your mouth and on your tongue. This doesn't happen overnight. To get rid of morning breath, brush your teeth or eat breakfast to send your spit back to work.

GROSS FACT

The first toothbrush was invented in China in 1498. The bristles were hair from pigs.

DROOL FACTORY

Babies make tons of extra spit. It covers their chins, clothes, and anything they put in their mouths — which is almost everything they touch. This excess spit is called drool.

In the past, people thought babies drooled because new teeth were poking through their gums. This is partly true. Babies often put toys and other objects in their mouths when they are teething. Chewing tricks the salivary glands into thinking that the baby is eating. This causes the glands to shoot out more spit.

Most scientists now believe that babies also drool because their bodies are getting ready for solid food. But babies aren't as good at swallowing spit as older people are. It pools in their mouths and trickles down their chins.

Babies aren't the only ones who don't always swallow their spit. Fall asleep with your mouth open, and you too could wake up in a puddle of drool!

Teething babies can practice chewing by gnawing on mushy foods like bananas.

A NASTY HABIT

Spit is 98 percent water.

Spit really is a miracle fluid. Speaking and eating would be impossible without it. Your teeth would probably be full of cavities too. Inside of you, spit is a wonderful thing. So why does it get such a bad rap when you shoot it out of your body?

Think about stepping in a blob of spit on the sidewalk or wiping up a baby's drool. Gross, huh? Spit is your body's buddy. But most people still think it's pretty nasty. And they've got good reasons for this opinion.

SNOT AND SPIT

You've probably seen – and heard – people snort up snot from their throats and spit out loogies. What are these disgusting blobs made of?

When you have a cold, snot, or mucus, builds up in your nose. One of the most natural places for this snot to go is down your throat. In this case, saliva helps get the job done. Your snot mixes with spit, and the mixture slips down your throat to your stomach.

Another way to get rid of snot is to push it up from your throat and into your mouth. Then you can use your amazing salivary powers to spit it out. Of course, that will probably gross out anyone standing near you.

GROSS FACT

Mucus is usually clear in color. But when a lot of bacteria is present, snot can be yellow or green.

Bacteria live in the mucus you blow out of your nose.

RUDE AND CRUDE

So is spitting really nasty? Or is it just something that grosses people out? Most scientists agree that spit is actually pretty gross. Your spit is full of bacteria. If you're sick, it's full of other germs too. In fact, germs can show up in your spit before you even feel sick. You can spread these germs to other people by coughing, sneezing, and spitting. Other people don't want to share the bacteria and germs swimming in your saliva.

Your body is covered in bacteria. Most are harmless, but some can cause serious illnesses.

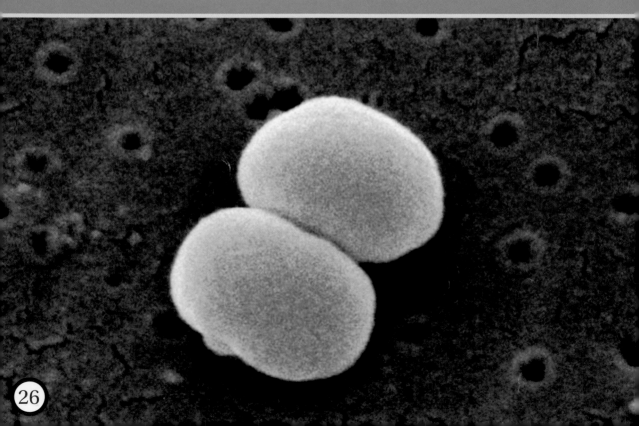

DOGGIE DROOL

Have you ever seen a cat or dog licking its wounds? It seems gross, but substances in some animals' spit help their wounds heal quicker.

Some scientists think human saliva might have this ability too. They are studying a substance in our spit that might help heal burns and other serious injuries.

But in the meantime, don't try this for yourself. Most scientists still argue that spit is full of germs that could get in your wounds and make you sick.

Besides landing you in the principal's office, spitballs are just plain gross!

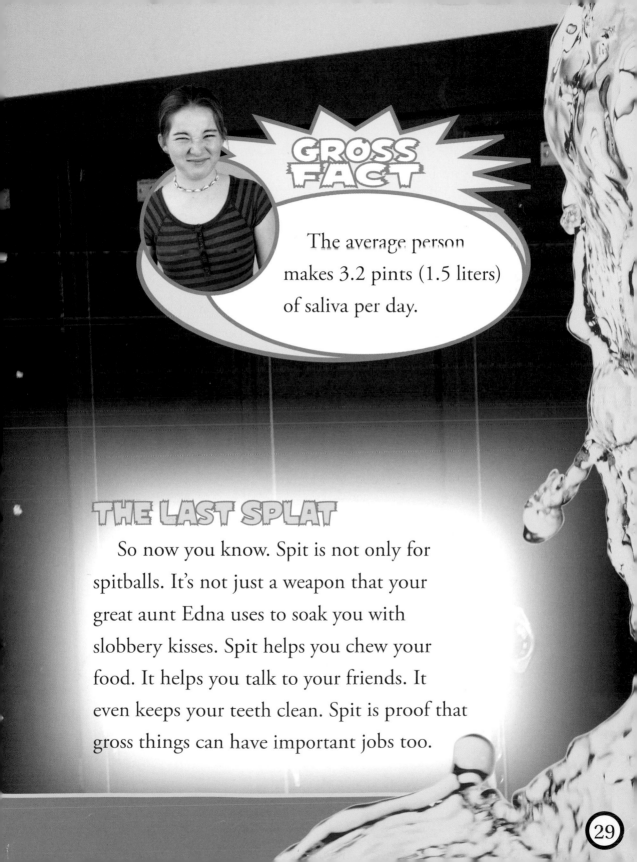

The average person makes 3.2 pints (1.5 liters) of saliva per day.

THE LAST SPLAT

So now you know. Spit is not only for spitballs. It's not just a weapon that your great aunt Edna uses to soak you with slobbery kisses. Spit helps you chew your food. It helps you talk to your friends. It even keeps your teeth clean. Spit is proof that gross things can have important jobs too.

GLOSSARY

acid (A-suhd) — a strong liquid; acids help break down food for energy.

allergies (A-luhr-jeez) — reactions to things that are harmless to most people, such as foods, pets, or dust

bacteria (bak-TEER-ee-uh) — one-celled, tiny organisms that can be found throughout nature; many bacteria are useful, but some cause disease.

bolus (BOHL-us) — a ball of food and saliva that travels down your throat to your stomach

cavity (KA-vuh-tee) — a decayed or broken down part of a tooth

enzyme (EN-zime) — a substance that helps break down food

esophagus (i-SAH-fuh-guhss) — the tube that carries food from the mouth to the stomach; muscles in the esophagus push food into the stomach.

gland (GLAND) — an organ that produces chemicals or substances that are used by the body

READ MORE

Gould, Francesca. *Why You Shouldn't Eat Your Boogers and Other Useless or Gross Information About Your Body.* New York: Penguin, 2008.

Stewart, Melissa. *It's Spit-acular!: the Secrets of Saliva.* The Gross and Goofy Body. New York: Marshall Cavendish Benchmark, 2009.

Szpirglas, Jeff, and Michael Cho. *Gross Universe: Your Guide to All Disgusting Things Under the Sun.* Toronto, Canada: Maple Tree Press, 2005.

INTERNET SITES

FactHound offers a safe, fun way to find Internet sites related to this book. All of the sites on FactHound have been researched by our staff.

Here's all you do:

Visit *www.facthound.com*

FactHound will fetch the best sites for you!

INDEX